Resting Place

poems by

Theresa Hickey

Finishing Line Press
Georgetown, Kentucky

Resting Place

Resting Place

"Be still and know that I am God." Psalm 46

"You have made us for yourself, oh Lord, and our hearts are restless until they rest in you." St. Augustine, Confessions

It's not always easy—carving out time for prayer and quiet and "doing nothing," but over time, the practice creates a calming space where I can catch a breath and draw a little closer to God. Soon, I notice a sense of well being as this practice, which may be new to some, begins to feel right. Surprisingly, I've begun to want the same for others, too—freedom from the chaos that burdens. Resting in the Lord's presence helps me decide which activities cause me to be scattered, anxious and restless— which choices place a desire in my heart for harmony and a little peace. There's no need to always sit in a chair to center myself. I can simply take a walk or do as Jesus did—go to the mountains or to the shore or to a favorite place in my mind, apart from distractions.

I began the practice of resting in God's presence when I was a young mother mostly absorbed by the formidable task of raising a family. Often, when I rested, I was so tired that I'd fall fast asleep. "How pathetic," I thought but I kept trying. The idea of sitting quietly, reading the Scriptures and contemplating its words was a bit odd at first, but I did want to know more about my faith and how it might help with the task of raising the family.

This was true of my husband, too. Soon, we were participating in a Bible study group—the Word of God ministry—and awakening each day wanting to pray and praise God. Seeking His presence brought unifying and hopeful ideas for whatever might lie ahead for us and our family. Slowly but surely, we were learning how the Holy Spirit was at work guiding us to a healthier realization of love for each other and others. It was far from the boring experience I imagined.

Inspiration from reading and praying the Scriptures brought about an outpouring of thanksgiving and a precious, new appreciation of people, places and things.. This is how *Resting Place* came to be—the ideas surfacing as a means of comfort and encouragement. They were uplifting to me while others who read them said they noticed a difference in their daily interactions, too. I began to believe that these poetic meditations were meant to do good and to be "a tender gift to the weary soul."*

"You have not chosen me, but I have chosen you, and have appointed you that you should go and bear fruit, and that your fruit should remain." (John 1, 5:16) St. Augustine, commenting on this verse, says that "this is an ineffable grace for if he had been the one to choose this relationship, it would have come from the nothingness of (his) human will and therefore lack the strength of divine mercy and the sureness of infallible wisdom." Augustine recognizes that without resting and being still in the Lord's presence, he is weak and unfulfilled. It is this alignment with the Spirit that ultimately led him and leads us toward greater understanding and resolve. Like Augustine, as we submit to inspirational promptings, we discover who we are meant to be. God's Word becomes a light we can depend upon.

God loves us and wants us to be happy. His amazing grace surrounds— every minute of every day.. When we prayerfully attempt to live in the moment, we see that our love adapts in ways which astonish.. All because He's chosen us and placed a desire in our hearts to take a little time each day for reflection—to be still and rest in Him.

*Leah Maines, commenting on *SHY*, Theresa Hickey's prior book of poetry. (2020)

Becoming

Through Him
With Him
In Him

Through Him
With Him
In Him

Through Him
With Him
In Him

ACKNOWLEDGMENTS

I'm grateful to the following publications who have featured my poems:

Shanti Arts ("Dance of the Butterfly")
The Florida Weekly ("Haiku Signs")
Lifespan: Turning the Corner, New Horizons ("The Healer")

Publisher: Leah Huete de Maines
Editor: Christen Kincaid
Cover Art: Rob Mulally on Unsplash
Cover Design: Elizabeth Maines McCleavy
Author's Family Photo: Oscar Gouveia

Order online: www.finishinglinepress.com
also available on Amazon.com and other book stores
Author inquiries and mail orders:
Finishing Line Press
PO Box 1626
Georgetown, Kentucky 40324
USA

Contents

"Arise and Walk" *

The world is
small sometimes
like a shoebox . . where
there is barely room
for air; where we feel
stifled, alone; yet, somehow
we inhale—we exhale—
we stumble, but do not fall
            Even on days fraught
with uncertainty—when
understanding is dark
as a charcoal sky—we
persist in our advocacy
toward wholeness

            Remember a time
when children—others
became saviors?
They needed
to be fed—to be clothed
to be comforted
to be taught, so
            Through days of milk
and medicine, as stale sighs
of fever flowed
into nights
of fitful sleep—
we inhaled; we exhaled—
we stumbled, but did not fall

            How is it that on days like this
when the world is small
like a shoebox. . .
days when we think that
thoughts might annihilate,
rob sobriety, we rise
to envision hope-filled vistas?

This is the power of the Resurrection!

*John 5:8 "Jesus said to him, pick up your mat and walk."

At the Athenaeum

Messengers of life's lessons
sit on the periphery
not wanting to enter in
unless opportunity knocks

Seated among us
are wordsmiths and scholars
each to recount
what they'd written that day

At the Athenaeum
we gather
to express how our poems
might give credence to life

We sit in a circle
to my right and left—
expressive, bright faces
like beacons of light

I wait.
I wonder.

What words could I offer?
What words might I say?

After the silence—
writing time over
each takes a turn
speaking poems aloud

"Metaphorically speaking
provocative, compelling."
I hear these superlatives
encircling the room

Each utterance spoken
literary works—lauded
each sees the other
as thoughtful, profound

What words could I offer?
What words might I say?

As my turn approaches
I tense; my brow furrows
I wish that the ground
could just swallow me up

"It's not ready" I sputter
"Too narrow; too predictable.
My poem is not ready—
 not ready just yet."

They wait.
They ponder.

"Hmmmm" says one poet
his hand cupping his chin
"Your words are not ready—
not ready just yet?"

". . . not ready. I sputter.
"Too hackneyed—Too staid.
My poem is not ready—
.not ready just yet."

A bearded man nods—
"It's not honed. It's not flawless?
Don't let that stop you
from speaking, my friend."

His words—empathetic—
heartfelt—endearing
a much-needed balm
for my timid, shy soul

I learned something that day
as I strove to do better—
"Do not let the perfect
be the enemy of good."*

*Idiom attributed to Voltaire (1770)

Breadth of Spring

When the colors of October pale
and winter blots the mind
with icy blasts,
like clockwork
our yearning begins; we long for
thawing interludes
mindfulness and purity—
a time when faith
revisits the unbeliever

In the chirping of birds
in the scent of mown grass;
in each manifestation
of lavender and pink—
artistic splendor
anoints the landscape
cracking open
our hearts

Spring, you are unlike any other
season. From dawn
to dusk, you restore
the down-trodden. Regaling
redemption in each
budding presence—
so that the blind embrace
sensibilities you tote

It is on days like this
so pregnant
with possibilities
that you magnify
the Creator
as all the earth affirms
the Promised Land

Castles in the Mangroves
(Dedicated to Pelican Bay friends and neighbors)

Walled by mangroves'
interwoven tapestries
shades of light rise, fall
upon each leafy limb

Their shadows form
a pageantry as breezes
rustle plumaged birds
saluting passersby

Ibis, pure as calla lillies,
Egrets, tall
and Herons, Little Blue,
are couriers. Common

Moorhens and brown Pelicans,
jester-like Anhingas,
Double-crested Cormorants,
reign as members of the court

A Cardinal's song spills
music from a distant tree
awakening all to morn's reverie,
and while embracing all as gift

I raise my eyes to wish, perhaps,
a crown, as white clouds
part above my head
revealing a blue diadem of sky

Though no storybook heiress lives here
no princess of royal blood,
all ours is this.
All this is ours

Dream Weavers

For Katrina and Caela, Annette and Ben, Gigi, Vera and Nina

Sun gives way to slumber
but doesn't reawaken
until you hail its arousal
yielding your wands. Once golden
rays spill onto your faces
your are deemed princes
or fairies or trolls
who govern the forest
with magic pinwheels

Adorned with boas, tiaras,
sceptors, crowns
you make ready the day—
the dreamers, pretenders,
wide-eyed believers
spin castles from flowers
cast spells from the soil

With eyes all aglow—you children—
all children—visit the beauty
of every small thing, You are
curators of mansions,
painters of rainbows. Curiosity
swirls from
your mind's carousels

Taller than shade trees
are the beams of your fortresses,
your hearts imaginings
richer than gold. You surely must see
that God sent you to teach me
that i may learn from your wonderment
follow your guise

Flowers in the Rain

Neverlands of lost boys,
winged fairies of imagination
the knowable—the unknowable—all
have been ours; mystery forever
spawns in us—creativity, too. We swim
same unchartered waters as before,
grateful now for islands of retreat

When chaos clamors
to befriend, we find comfort
in the pages of a favorite book;
despite fears, we rise
above mountaintops
needing little more than
miniscule views from the top

Should we spin
out of control,
we bend toward silence
becoming grounded
like plantings, deep-rooted—
seeking buffers against
raging winds

Finding enough in the everyday,
sleep soothes; some nights
we languish
as if afloat upon the sea,
listening closely
to its murmurs; no longer
plunging in, we wade

We have become flowers
in the rain—a resilient people
rising upward
to meet the sun's rays
uplifted—even though
sadness, grief lie
burrowed within

Athough we say—
"all child's play"
each dream—each game
has taught us well
that joy is formed from mustard seeds—
that heaven sends envoys
with small torch lights
in our wakes,
and love—love,
centered in our spirits
whispered in our prayers—is
every-ready to lead us home

H A I K U—Signs

Above the lawn flies
Your red kite furling breezes
Helps loneliness flee

Pressed lips upon glass
Traced against locked doors reveal
Smudges of our past

Birds on wing remind
Today's dirge shall pass away
Raise us to new heights

(May, 2020—Written during the Pandemic) Published in *Florida Weekly*

"I Will Still Love You"

On the day I leave this earth
there could be
a spectacle in the sky—
fireworks beyond description,
an aurora borealis
in the night, so do not be
too sad, too long. I am around—
in someplace new, and
I'll be trying to say,
"I still love you"
If I see that you
shed tears, I'll collect them
in a jar—to make green
the grasses of your garden
despite summer's heat. I'll be trying
to let you know—to say,
"Don't worry. I still love you"
Should you miss my voice
in the hours after I kiss the world goodbye
open a window—
applause may fill the void
like a curtain call. Maybe I will paint
bold murals across the sky
on the rooftop of my new home
because it may be grander
than we thought and may make you smile
for I still love you
Lastly, if you should hear
calming refrains of Pachelbel's *Canon*—
an echo of my parting gift—
or see swarms of humming bees
or a tree whose foliage surprises
after many seasons of not blooming
these things will assure you
"Yes. . . it's me,
and I still love you"
Look for sights and sounds like these
as you seek me among the living, like
two rabbits in a field, perhaps,
as when Papa died, or in the yellow
glint of flitting butterflies

for if there is a way—a way to you
I'll find it—to speak my mind—to let you know—
"No need for fear; I am here and. . .
Oh, how I still love you"

In Search of Sanctuary

My mother walked with her mother
through this neighboring cemetery.
Now as I trace their steps,
I linger along the cement pavement
of this burial ground—
seeking answers when questions arise
about death, dying, what matters in life.

Here lie the remains of,
influential people—oridinary people. We
did not know them, but at one time,
they may have tried
to be as present to others
as my mother's mother was to her
as my mother was to me.

Passing tall, resilient evergreens,
I wonder if the bodies of departed—
their spines, their shoulders,
were strong
when life burdened.

I hope these loved ones
did not see their earthly days
as bleak, restricted, gray
as these tombs,
bound by granite stones.

Each small plaque
each flag, commemorative
cherub is a small momento left by one
who, for better or worse,
misses the departed—
revisits the past,
inhabits the loss.

Perhaps this ground
where every mother's child
now rests
holds mysterious sanctions
in the greenery—

in the air
once breathed.

     One day our spirit selves
will soar beyond
the imaginable
as do these Birches, Elms and Maples
where, above each crypt,
branches raise
unspoken dreams.

     The arbors sway
with every gentle breeze,
longing with us
in us, for us—
for a day when we need not
plod along among ruins
in search of sanctuary.

     Then, we will *be* the place
where malice cannot harm, where true love
calls our names, where joy
can know no bounds,
where freedom reigns
and mothers' prayers
come full circle.

In the Butterfly Garden

Nature releases butterflies
      to wake us from our sleep
            to give birth to dreams

Tiny emissaries,
      seemingly of little consequence,
            invite us to envision peaceful possibilities

With delicate thrusts, they
      propel motion—buoyantly,
            as though possessing heavenly spirits

They float and career over rocks
      and ridges, grasses and flora, darting just as sprightly
            along dusty roads as green meadows

Soaring ever so lightly from the ordinary
      into the realm of the magical, their ethereal presence
            reveals the grace of a grander scheme

As a child,
      I tried to capture butterflies in a net, contain them
            in a jar; their frail wings did not give me pause

To imagine how fragile their flight—
      how wrong my attempts
            to snatch them from the landscape

Rising skyward above green trees
      or alighting on the dew-grass of summer
            the butterfly's message
is carried to the earthbound:

            ~ Living is a delicate freedom ~

"In the Butterfly Garden" was originally published by *Still Points Arts Quarterly* (2020)

Morning Bells . . .

ring out the dawn of a new day
as I walk the half-mile from home to St. Mary's.
they draw me in,
they raise me up
they impel the prayers of a silent heart

Their chimes ring out
to rouse me
from my drowsiness
as I stroll along deserted roads,
lit by lamp lights

Faith begins to stir as
day begins, while
at the same time a prayer
to seek forgiveness rises—
"Please help my unbelief"

For those who are grateful—
for those unaware—the bells toll.
They remind me of my need to serve,
to let go of every pressing thought;
let go of everything that seems
too hard to bear

Soon I'll kneel to lean on—
learn to trust the Spirit within—small
ways to bring kindness
to friends and friendless—
to offer rightful praise
before nightfall steals the day

I mount the steps as
compelling peals beckon
me to listen—to listen
not to speak—
to pay attention to what is—
to what may be customarily overlooked
like mud beneath my boots,

like the man who sits,
head bowed, unable to rise
to take Communion

Morning bells seek metanoia—
a change of mind and heart
Am I open? Am I ready
to quell the ringing of the bells?

Ode to Mary Lee

Many things from the past
were worn and woven
into our beings like ideas from
books you gave us—
gifts on our birthdays. From your first
few words written in ink
on opening pages, we
knew you believed in us—
in our ability to learn, to ruminate, to
ask the right questions of the world

It didn't matter that we came
from families of immigrants
who lived simply and unobtrusively
who didn't know much about
the political arena or affairs
of the world. In your mind
we were a capable presence—
so you led us to savor
words, to persevere,
to seek change

When you spoke of world
leaders, historians, writers,
philosophers, artists
of different cultures from
distant shores, your face
would shine; your voice
would elevate in adulation
as if these greats of bygone
eras were being made
manifest through you

I won't mention your full name—
that would be too much for you—
to think that someone may discover
things about you that you would
rather leave unsaid—but
to all in your classroom—even
on those bleak February days
when everyone wanted to stay

in bed, your efforts made us
glad when we showed up

That's what it was like—
hearing you speak—
being invited
to your banquet table

That's what it was like—
growing up in a poor neighborhood
but thinking that we
were rich kids

Once our imaginations sparked,
it was like spring's thaw
after harrowing snows;
our hearts raced

Thanks to you,
many things from the past
worn and woven
into our beings remain—
seemingly etched there
for all time

One with the Seasons

As seasons unfold,
they introduce themselves
with unparalleled regalia,
centering into our lives
bearing gifts

Summer days give pause
so that tiny measures
of hot breaths seep
into our veins
with rains that water soil

Autumn flaunts her veils
scattering warmth to wind;
a wandering gypsy,
her farewells provoke
an impassioned presence

The thickest of blankets
buffer against bitter blasts of winter,
but soon, we long for
open doors of springtime—
her vigor, her vitality

When spring finally arrives,
blossoms are delivered
on her wings; their fragrance—
whimsical in the air—
all sweetness and surrender

Such are the ways of the seasons—
how mysterious to watch
as they lie in wait, entering in
with temperaments
like our own—

They are with us,
in us, through us
like the very God
who makes us
One

Praise of the Swallow

A short-feathered bird casts its demeanor
across the summer sky. She has flown
from the North, across a stretch of beach,
a fluttering of deft wings
above a cascading sea

I cannot take my eyes from her—
a little urchin heading along a path
she navigates with surety. She
becomes small, smaller, speck-
on-sky as she winnows into wind

The sky absorbs her into its bosom
but does not crack open
or spin out of control. It does not
spawn a divide or
display any seam of entry

Further pondering her flight,
I watch and wait a long time,
sad to see her fly away, hoping
an act of will may bring her back
but someone across the vast horizon
stretches to gaze upon her, too,
with anticipation, appreciation—
this tiny creature revels
in fullness of flight
with every wavering of her wings

Respect

       During my daily walk, I watch
as a smattering of starlings gather
for breakfast along the curb,
pecking at crumbs
tossed from a neighbor's window.
Creatures of habit, most mornings,
we show up
       The creek rushes
with uproarious clamor today, filled
beyond measure
after last night's rainfall—
intent on showing off;
no time
to slow her pace
       An entourage of critters awaken
across the footbridge
as the morning sun opens
its gaze. I rub noses
with summery flora
stylishly adorned
in May dresses
       Ducks in random
formations align
coastal marshlands;
they preen and meander
from woodland fonts;
mindful of my passing,
they call to one another
       I'm new to these neighborhoods
but inhabitants
among marshy reeds,
welcome me—they
do not view me
as a stranger
as an intruder
       I have much to learn from wild life—
from every tree and shrub, grace
abides to show its face as
each protege of nature
shifts to befriend me, showing
me a road less traveled—
a more docile way to tread

Secrets of the Sun and Moon

As you illuminate the morning
and probe the mind, we understand
a little of the exceptional

You embolden the good
storing it like gold
when the landscape is bleak

You are a stronghold of the Spirit,
safegaurding gifts for a time
ripe for dispensing

When we aspire to act on a thought that is beyond
comprehension, you fix
our gaze on the unimaginable

With tiny sparks
you emblazon
the universe

Soulful Sun. . . you spur the brightness of day
bringing energy to our limbs,
vitality to dry bones

Mystical Moon . . . . you rise
to every occasion with
same faithfulness

You spawn the easiness of sleep
bringing calm
to our fragile beings

Above tree tops, valleys
ridges, plains, your embrace
surrounds all, rapt in your beams

Light from your throne
entreats cornfields and pastures
spilling their bounty; nourishing the throngs

You are haunting indeed,
on those summer-lit nights,
deep is your counsel surpassing the rest

While you glow through the darkness
days' worries dwindle
angels keep watch with promises of grace

Dispelling the shadows amid swells
of your face, you rise to enlighten;
fears fly away

From dark tapestries your face shines
seeking peace through the shadows
showering wisdom
while the world takes its rest

We give thanks for each glorious day, Sister Sun
We give thanks for the star-studded night, Brother Moon

Mother Earth, mid your splendor,
we, awe-struck and silent,
praise all of creation, born of
beauty and light
in the power of your presence
there is hope for all seasons
strength for our days

Seductress

A diamond necklace
shines upon the sea's bosom
in brilliant bursts of sunlight
wispy clouds
form ringlets about
her radiant face

In the afterglow
of an agate morning
she dances
her ritual
of timeless renewal,
her energy pulses;
minutes become hours

When night's starkness
gives pause for rendezvous,
she languishes in the arms
of a mischievous moon
as together they listen
to incantations of the Sirens
enamored as was Odysseus
by sounds emanating far and deep

Crescendos resonate
from within her depths,
calling across a wide expanse
of time and place, echoing
the ardor within those of us
forever lost within her charms

Solace

In crevices that cross the brow

In the pelting of a springtime rain

Ablaze in rays of summer's heat

When windblown hair

Lashes against wet cheeks

In the silence of the midnight hour

When tears lament and words empower
an unexpected phrase

In coupled hands
When courage wanes

By gifts imbued
With a sweet surprise
Or a special refrain

Close as skin, as skin on bone—

Our loved ones, gone, yet

With us, just the same,

The love of our dearly—departed—

Remains

We, forever beholden of that face

Spirit's Song

Speak it softly

Speak it sweetly

Speak it in the hush of morn

In the noon hour

In the evening

When endeavors are forlorn

Speak it boldly

From the rafters

Speak as if

The end draws near

From your heart store

Faith will muster

Bending loved ones to their knees

We wait in stalwart intercessions

While our Lord-God parts the seas

The Healer

There is power in actions that break our hearts.
There is power in stories that cut.
There is power in words which cast doubt or blame.
There is power in the events we don't wish to recount.
Be Still
Arise from your sleep.
How will we know there is light, there is love
When thoughts betray all that is good?
Look to the past, past this torment of grief
and remember the manifold ways
God restores us, renews us,
Dries tears from our eyes
To ground us in love once again

"The Healer" was originally published in *Lifespan: Turning the Corner*, New Horizons (2023)

The Summons

Saints and sinners—one—
know it's never about perfection—
more the searching and the trying
the losing and the persevering
the giving up and giving in
the waiting and the hoping
the patience of embracing that which is
and that which may come to pass

We awaken—we rise
we "live and breathe
and have our being"* each morning
 each evening—so when
our lives give pause—granting
glimpses of holiness in the mundane—
we see that in days of famine or harvest
in the unexpected and serendipitous
in the yeses and nos we profess,
we are asked to grapple
with the choices
that redefine love

*Acts: 17:28 "In Him we live and move and have our being. . ."

Waiting for the Sunrise

In grandeur high above an awakening earth,
sun rises against a sleepy sky
as I must
I need the mercy of the morning to direct my steps—
to breathe deeply
from her coffers
A contented bird spills a love song into day
to soothe mind and spirit like agile fingers
skimming harp strings
As sunshine warms to fill the room
my uplifted face seeks assurances
against yesterday's omissions
Will inspiration awaken like the droplets that glisten
upon leafy branches
outside my window?
There *is* harmony where earth and sky
and woodland meet, their simple presence—
perfect as a prayer, yet
My being knows a subtle yearning
at this silent hour
like the whimpering of a child—
lowly groans within
a constricted temple
longing for another day's empowerment

"All I ask of you is to forever remember me as loving you."

Gregory Norbet (Lyrics of Catholic hymn)

Theresa Hickey (center) is pictured with her husband, Michael, surrounded by their four children, their children's spouses and seven grandchildren.

Theresa Hickey is an award-winning poet and free-lance writer whose prior books include *Raising the Child, Sighs of a Gracious Nature* and *Shy*, published by Finishing Line Press (2020). *Shy* was awarded a 2021 Poetry Book Award by the Catholic Media Association of the U.S. and Canada. Boston Globe Book Reviewer, Nina MacLaughlin, has praised her work and compared it to Mary Oliver's: "The author focuses on life devoted to an ongoing search and questions of spirituality and faith . . . . 'life lived in union with Spirit.'" Her work has appeared in *Still Point Arts Quarterly, New England Memories, Halcyon Days, FaithND (Notre Dame), NatureWriting, Lifespan* and other anthologies.

As a participant and former leader of the Pelican Bay Women's League Writers, Theresa encourages the writing and spiritual growth of others. She is a 40-year participant in a meditation group where she continues to study and share insights from sacred Scriptures which inspire her poems.

She is retired from her work as a Salem State University administrator and has been married to husband/author Michael for 59 years; they have four children and seven grandchildren. Proceeds from her books support food pantries and other nonprofits. You can reach her at theresadhickey@gmail.com.